Stage 5 Pack A

Floppy's Phonics
Fiction

Kate Ruttle

Group/ ...es

Contents

The Gale

Please Do Not Sneeze

The Missing Crystal

Rowing Boats

Mr Scroop's School

The Haunted House

Introduction

Welcome to *Floppy's Phonics!* This series gives you decodable phonic stories featuring all your favourite *Oxford Reading Tree* characters. The books provide the perfect opportunity for consolidation and practice of synthetic phonics within a familiar setting, to build your children's confidence. As well as having a strong phonic focus, each story is a truly satisfying read with lots of opportunities for comprehension, so they are fully in line with the simple view of reading.

Phonic development

The *Floppy's Phonics* Stage 5 stories support a synthetic phonics approach to early reading skills and are fully aligned to *Letters and Sounds*. They should be used for practice and consolidation. The books should be read in the suggested order (see chart on page 3), so that children can benefit from the controlled introduction, revision and consolidation of the phonemes. They can be used before the *Floppy's Phonics Non-fiction* books at the same stage. In addition, they can be used for practice and consolidation after introducing the sounds with other programmes.

The series can be used by children working within Phase 5 of *Letters and Sounds*, to support them as they broaden their knowledge of graphemes and phonemes for use in reading and spelling. The books will help to embed these vital early phonics skills, and help to ensure that children will experience success in learning to read and thus will be motivated to keep on reading.

Your children will benefit most from reading *Floppy's Phonics* Stage 5 if they are able to:

- read and spell words containing adjacent consonants
- read some phonically decodable two and three syllable words with increasing confidence
- recognize the *Letters and Sounds* high frequency words for Phases 4 and 5
- begin to recognize new graphemes and alternative pronunciations of these, and of the graphemes they already know.

Phonic focus

This chart shows which Phase 5 phonemes are introduced and practised in each title.

Title	ORT Stage Book band colour Year group	*Letters and Sounds* phase	Phonic focus	Phonemes revisited
The Gale	Stage 5 Green Y1/ P2	Phase 5	/ai/ ay ai a-e eigh ey /f/ f ph Alternative pronunciations of "u" (put (south), but)	Phase 4 adjacent consonants Phase 3 graphemes
Please Do Not Sneeze	Stage 5 Green Y1/ P2	Phase 5	/ee/ ea y ee ie ey e e-e eo /e/ e ea Alternative pronunciations of "er" (better, her) "y" (you, story, by)	Phase 4 adjacent consonants Phase 3 graphemes
The Missing Crystal	Stage 5 Green Y1/ P2	Phase 5	/igh/ igh i-e y -ie- /i/ y /ur/ ir er ear ur Alternative pronunciations of "o" (hot, gold) "i" (wind, find)	Phase 4 adjacent consonants Phase 3 graphemes
Rowing Boats	Stage 5 Green Y1/ P2	Phase 5	/oa/ oa oe o-e ow o /oi/ oi oy Alternative pronunciations of "y" (yes, by, very)	Phase 4 adjacent consonants Phase 3 graphemes
Mr Scroop's School	Stage 5 Green Y1/ P2	Phase 5	/oo/ oo u-e ue ew ui ou /er/ er e a o Alternative pronunciations of "ow" (how, show)	Phase 4 adjacent consonants Phase 3 graphemes
The Haunted House	Stage 5 Green Y1/ P2	Phase 5	/or/ au aw al or our /oo/ ou oo u o /o/ (w)a o Alternative pronunciations of "c" (cellar, could) "a" (that, what)	Phase 4 adjacent consonants Phase 3 graphemes

Vocabulary

High frequency words are words which occur frequently in children's books. Many of them are decodable, some of them are "tricky". The words are defined in line with *Letters and Sounds*.

Decodable words

Most of the common words introduced in *Floppy's Phonics* are phonically decodable, using phonic skills and knowledge that is gradually developed through the series.

Tricky words

Tricky words are words which contain unusual grapheme-phoneme correspondences (e.g. *we, they*). The advice in *Letters and Sounds* is that children should be taught to recognize the phonemes they know within these words and to distinguish these from the tricky bits. For example, in the word *they*, children should be taught to recognize the grapheme *th* and then taught the tricky sound of 'ey' in this context.

High frequency words used in each book

The Gale	Decodable words	came day make
	Tricky words	called their people
Please Do Not Sneeze	Decodable words	came house(s) here
	Tricky words	people called looked their
The Missing Crystal	Decodable words	very
	Tricky words	called asked
Rowing Boats	Decodable words	came here by very
	Tricky words	asked their oh could called
Mr Scroop's School	Decodable words	don't very your time(s)
	Tricky words	Mr Mrs called asked oh could their
The Haunted House	Decodable words	don't house saw old here very
	Tricky words	oh asked

Comprehension Strategies

Reading is about making meaning, and it is particularly important that a child's earliest reading books offer opportunities for making meaning and telling a complete story. As with all *Oxford Reading Tree* stories, the titles in *Floppy's Phonics* are fun stories which children will really enjoy, and which will give you lots of scope for practising and extending their comprehension skills.

Story	Comprehension strategy taught through these Group/Guided Reading Notes				
	Prediction	Questioning	Clarifying	Summarizing	Imagining
The Gale	✓		✓	✓	✓
Please Do Not Sneeze	✓		✓		✓
The Missing Crystal	✓	✓	✓		✓
Rowing Boats	✓	✓	✓	✓	✓
Mr Scroop's School			✓	✓	✓
The Haunted House	✓		✓		✓

Curriculum coverage charts

	Speaking, Listening, Drama	Reading	Writing
The Gale			
PNS Literacy Framework (Y1)	1.1	**W** 5.2, 5.5, 6.5 **C** 7.4	9.5
National Curriculum	Working within level 1		
Scotland: Curriculum for Excellence (P2)	First Level: LIT 102B, 107G, 109J, 110K ENG 103C	First Level: LIT 112N, 113P, 119V	First Level: LIT 120X, 121Y, 123AA
N. Ireland (P2)	1, 2, 3, 4, 6, 7, 10, 11, 13, 14	1, 2, 3, 5, 8, 9, 15, 17	1, 2, 3, 4, 5, 6, 7, 9, 11, 12, 14
Wales (Key Stage 1)	Skills: 1, 2, 3, 5, 6, 7, 8, 9 Range: 1, 2, 3, 4, 5, 6, 7	Skills: 1, 3, 4, 5, 6, 7, 8 Range: 2, 3, 4, 5, 6	Skills: 2, 3, 4, 5, 6, 7, 8, 9, 10, 13 Range: 1, 2, 3, 4, 5
Please Do Not Sneeze			
PNS Literacy Framework (Y1)	4.2	**W** 5.2, 5.3, 5.4 **C** 7.4	11.1
National Curriculum	Working within level 1		
Scotland: Curriculum for Excellence (P2)	First Level: LIT 102B, 107G, 110K	First Level: LIT 112N, 113P, 117T ENG 119V	First Level: LIT 120X, 121Y, 123AA, 125AC
N. Ireland (P2)	1, 2, 3, 4, 5, 7, 11, 14	1, 2, 3, 5, 6, 8, 9, 14, 15, 16, 17	1, 2, 3, 4, 5, 6, 7, 9, 10, 11, 12
Wales Key Stage 1	Skills: 1, 2, 3, 5, 6, 7, 8, 10, 12, 13 Range: 1, 2, 3, 4, 5, 6, 7	Skills: 1, 3, 4, 5, 7, 8 Range: 2, 3, 4, 5, 6	Skills: 1, 2, 3, 4, 5, 6, 7, 8, 9, 10, 13 Range: 1, 2, 3, 4, 5

Curriculum coverage charts

	Speaking, Listening, Drama	Reading	Writing
The Missing Crystal			
PNS Literacy Framework (Y1)	4.1	**W** 5.1, 5.2, 5.5 **C** 7.4	9.2
National Curriculum	Working within level 1		
Scotland: Curriculum for Excellence (P2)	First Level: LIT 102B, 110K ENG 103C	First Level: LIT 112N, 113P, 114Q ENG 19V	First Level: LIT 120X, 121Y, 122Z, 123AA
N. Ireland (P2)	1, 2, 3, 4, 5, 6, 7, 10, 13, 14	1, 2, 3, 4, 5, 8, 9, 13, 14, 15	1, 2, 3, 4, 7, 9, 11, 12
Wales Key Stage 1	Skills: 1, 2, 3, 4, 5, 6, 7, 8, 10, 12, 13 Range: 1, 2, 3, 4, 5, 6, 7	Skills: 1, 3, 4, 5, 6, 7, 8 Range: 2, 3, 4, 5, 6	Skills: 1, 2, 3, 4, 5, 6, 7, 8, 9, 10, 13 Range: 1, 2, 3, 4, 5
Rowing Boats			
PNS Literacy Framework (Y1)	4.1	**W** 5.1, 6.1, 6.4 **C** 7.4	10.1
National Curriculum	Working within level 1		
Scotland: Curriculum for Excellence (P2)	First Level: LIT 107G, 108H, 109J, 110K	First Level: LIT 112N, 113P, 112Q ENG 119V	First Level: LIT 120X, 125AC, 126 AE/AF
N. Ireland (P2)	1, 2, 3, 4, 5, 6, 8, 10	1, 2, 3, 4, 5, 8, 9, 14, 15, 16, 17	1, 2, 3, 4, 6, 9, 11, 12
Wales Key Stage 1	Skills: 1, 2, 3, 6, 7, 8, 9, 10, 12, 13 Range: 1, 2, 3, 4, 5, 6, 7	Skills: 1, 2, 3, 4, 5, 6, 7, 8 Range: 2, 3, 4, 5	Skills: 1, 2, 3, 5, 6, 7, 8, 9, 10, 13 Range: 1, 2, 3, 4, 5

Curriculum coverage charts

	Speaking, Listening, Drama	Reading	Writing
Mr Scroop's School			
PNS Literacy Framework (Y1)	1.2	**W** 5.1, 5.2, 6.5 **C** 8.3	11.1
National Curriculum	Working within level 1		
Scotland: Curriculum for Excellence (P2)	First Level: LIT 102B, 109J, 110K ENG 103C	First Level: LIT 112N, 113P ENG 119 V	First Level: LIT 120X, 121Y, 123AA, 125AC
N. Ireland (P2)	1, 2, 3, 4, 6, 7, 8, 10, 13, 14	1, 2, 3, 4, 5, 6, 8, 9, 13, 14, 15, 16, 17	1, 2, 3, 6, 7, 8, 9, 11, 12
Wales (Key Stage 1)	Skills: 1, 2, 3, 5, 6, 7, 12, 13 Range: 1, 2, 3, 4, 5, 6, 7	Skills: 1, 2, 3, 4, 5, 6, 7, 8 Range: 1, 2, 3, 4, 5, 6, 8, 9, 13, 14, 15, 16, 17	Skills: 1, 2, 3, 5, 6, 7, 8, 9, 10, 13 Range: 1, 2, 3, 6, 7, 9, 11, 12
The Haunted House			
PNS Literacy Framework (Y1)	4.1	**W** 5.1, 5.2, 6.1 **C** 8.2	9.1
National Curriculum	Working within level 1		
Scotland: Curriculum for Excellence (P2)	First Level: LIT 102B, 109J, 110K	First Level: LIT 112N, 113P ENG 119V	First Level: LIT 121Y, 122Z, 125AC ENG 128AH
N. Ireland (P2)	1, 2, 3, 4, 6, 7, 13, 14	1, 2, 3, 4, 5, 8, 14, 15, 16, 17	1, 2, 3, 4, 7, 11, 12
Wales (Key Stage 1)	Skills: 1, 2, 3, 6, 7, 8, 12, 13 Range: 1, 2, 3, 4, 5, 6, 7	Skills: 1, 3, 4, 5, 6, 7, 8 Range: 2, 3, 4, 5	Skills: 1, 2, 3, 5, 6, 7, 8, 9, 10, 13 Range: 1, 2, 3, 4, 5

The Gale

C = Language comprehension   **A** = Assessment

W = Word recognition   **O** = Objective

Guided or group reading

Phonic Focus:

New graphemes for reading: /ai/ –ay, ai, a–e, eigh, ey; /f/ f, ph
Alternative pronunciations: "u" in *put, south, but*
High frequency words: called, their, people, came, day, make

Introducing the book

W Can children read the title? Help them to recognize the split digraph a–e in *Gale*.

W Turn to page 1. How many words can children find with /ai/? Which words? How is /ai/ represented? (*ay* in *away, bay, holiday, staying* and *ey* in *they*; *a–e* in *place, ace*)

C *(Predicting)* Encourage children to use prediction: *What is a gale? What might happen in a gale?*

Look through the book, talking about what happens on each page. Use some of the high frequency words as you discuss the story (see chart on page 4).

Strategy check

Remind the children to sound the words out carefully, remembering to look to see if there is a split digraph 'e', as well as looking at adjacent letters in a word.

Independent reading

Ask children to read the story aloud. Praise and encourage them while they read, and prompt as necessary.

C *(Clarifying)* Ask children to tell you how the family kept safe in the storm.

Assessment Check that children:

- *(AF 1)* use phonic knowledge to sound out and blend the phonemes in words (see chart on page 3).
- *(AF 1)* recognize different ways of representing *ai*.
- *(AF 1)* recognize different pronunciations of *u*.
- *(AF 2 and 3)* use comprehension skills to work out what is happening.
- *(AF 1)* make a note of any difficulties the children encounter and of strategies they use to solve problems.

Returning to the text

(W) How many different ways of representing *ai* can the children remember?

Assessment *(AF 1)* Discuss any words the children found tricky and talk about strategies used.

Group and independent reading activities

Objective Recognize and use alternative ways of spelling the phonemes already taught (5.2).

(W) **You will need:** flashcards showing different ways of representing /ai/ ai, ay, a–e, eigh, ey; blank pieces of paper, for children to write words on.

- Read the book aloud to page 5. Ask children to raise their hands every time they hear the phoneme /ai/ in a word.
- Introduce the flashcards. Give pairs of children a number of pages in the book to look at. Ask children to find /ai/ words featuring each of the spelling patterns to make sets of words with the same spelling.
- Which letter pattern is used most often? Least often?

Assessment *(AF 1)* Can children hear the phoneme /ai/ in text and recognize some of the graphemes associated with it?

Objective Apply phonic knowledge and skills as the prime approach to reading and spelling unfamiliar words (5.5).

(W) **You will need:** flashcards with the real and nonsense words: *face, space, spale, grain, paint, staip, play, staying, grayn, they, grey, bley, eight, sleigh, jeigh*; a dustbin and a treasure chest.

- Put all of the words face down on the table.
- Remind children of the rules of the game: they take it in turns to turn over a word, read it, show it to others and decide whether it's a real word (treasure) or a made up word (rubbish).

Assessment *(AF 1)* Can children read the words successfully and make good decisions about whether they're real words or not?

Objective To identify constituent parts of two syllable words (6.5).

(W) Orally, count how many syllables there are in *Kipper, children, picture, extra, plastic, today, corner, began, ladder; Phil, gale, storm, howl, played.*

- Show children the words: *bucket, today, corner, began.* Can children draw lines to show where the syllable boundary occurs? (*plas/tic Kip/per, be/gan, corn/er*)
- Talk about the words: *starfish, loudhailer.* What's special about those words? Introduce the idea of compound words: words made up of two other words. Can children think of any more compound words?

Assessment *(AF 1)* Can children correctly identify the consonant boundary each time?

Objective Recognize the main elements that shape different texts (7.4).

(C) *(Summarizing)* Show three cards: *beginning, middle, end.*

- Ask children what happened at the beginning of the book.
- What happened in the middle.
- And what happened at the end.
- Encourage discussion about how much of the story can be included under each of the headings.

Assessment *(AF 4)* Can children explain their segmenting of the story into the different parts?

Speaking, listening and drama activities

Objective Tell stories and describe incidents from their own experience in an audible voice (1.1).

(C) *(Imagining)* Use the sandpit or water tray to re-create the storm in the book. Invite children to join in with descriptive words and dramatic voices.

● Add supplementary characters to your storm. They could be in tents or boats, or just watching the storm.

● Encourage children to empathize with the supplementary characters. What does it sound and feel like? If children have any personal experiences to share, encourage them to add these in too.

Assessment *(AF 6)* Can children contribute ideas and experiences to develop the group understanding of being in a storm?

Writing activities

Objective Create short simple texts on paper and on screen that combine words and images (and sounds) (9.5).

(C) *(Imagining)* Ask children to write on a computer about being in a storm.

● When they have composed their text, show them how to search on the internet for images and sounds to add to their text.

● Share the completed text with other children.

Assessment *(Writing AF 2)* Can children make appropriate choices about the language, images and sounds they use given the mode of writing they have selected?

Please Do Not Sneeze

> **C** = Language comprehension   **A** = Assessment
>
> **W** = Word recognition   **O** = Objective

Guided or group reading

Phonic Focus:

New graphemes for reading: /ee/ ea, y, ee, ie, ey, e, e–e, eo; /e/ e, ea
Alternative pronunciations: "er" in *harder, better, manners, her;* "y" in *you, story, by*
High frequency words: people, called, looked, their, came, house(s) here

Introducing the book

W Can children read the title? Help them to recognize both representations of /ee/.

W Turn to page 1. How many words can children find with /ee/? Which words? How is /ee/ represented? (*ee* in *Anneena, ea* in *sea, beach* and *y* as the final sound in *sunny* and *chilly*).

C *(Predicting)* Encourage children to use prediction: *What kinds of things happen when you sneeze? Why might someone ask you not to? What might happen in this story?*

Look through the book, talking about what happens on each page. Use some of the high frequency words as you discuss the story (see chart on page 4).

Strategy check

Remind the children to sound the words out carefully, remembering to look at adjacent letters in a word in case both are needed to represent a sound.

Independent reading

Ask children to read the story aloud. Praise and encourage them while they read, and prompt as necessary.

C *(Clarifying)* Ask children to tell you whether their predictions about what might happen were accurate.

Assessment Check that children:

- *(AF 1)* use phonic knowledge to sound out and blend the phonemes in words (see chart on page 3).
- *(AF 1)* recognize different ways of representing ee.
- *(AF 1)* recognize different pronunciations of *ea* and y.
- *(AF 2 and 3)* use comprehension skills to work out what is happening.
- *(AF 1)* make a note of any difficulties the children encounter and of strategies they use to solve problems.

Returning to the text

W Can children find words in which *ea* is pronounced in different ways?

Assessment *(AF 1)* Discuss any words the children found tricky and talk about strategies used.

Group and independent reading activities

Objective Identify constituent parts of two and three syllable words (5.3).

W Ask children to find what Princess Sophie said when she sneezed. Write the words.

- Look together at the list you have made. Clap the syllables as you read the list aloud. Talk about what all of the sayings have in common: e.g. always two words; always have an /ee/ somewhere; always a two syllable word followed by a one syllable word; the last sound of the first syllable always sounds a bit like /ee/; they're not polite things to say.
- Ask each pair of children to look closely at one of the two syllable words. Challenge them to sound out each syllable separately and to tell you where the syllable boundary is.
- Ask children to think of other things Princess Sophie might have said. Remind them of the pattern you have just uncovered.

Assessment *(AF 1)* Can children suggest new sayings that fit the same pattern?

Objective Recognize alternative ways of spelling phonemes already taught (5.2).

(W) You will need: flashcards with the words: *please, sneeze, Anneena, beach, sea, people, frisbee, Sophie, chilly, sunny, Lily, Charlie, Mummy.*

● Put all of the words on the table.

● First, ask the children to sort the words into two sets: where /ee/ sounds as it does in *sneeze* and where it sounds as it does in *Mummy.* Talk about how these two sounds are slightly different.

● Let different children work with each of the sets. They should circle the letters that represent /ee/ each time then look through the book to find more words with their kind of /ee/.

Assessment *(AF 1)* Can children hear /ee/ and identify the letters that represent it?

Objective To recognize automatically an increasing number of high frequency words (5.4).

(W) Tell the children you're going to ask them to re-read the book, searching for words that they think children in their class should learn to read. Remind them to look for words that can't be sounded out very easily.

● Look together at the first page. Can they see any words that can't be sounded out? *(was, the)* Ask them to read the rest of the book in pairs to find more words.

● Ask the children for ideas for remembering the words.

Assessment *(AF 1)* Can children identify words that can't be sounded out and suggest ways of remembering them?

Objective Find specific information in simple texts (7.4).

(C) *(Clarifying)* Each child should re-read the book and prepare two questions to ask others about what happened.

● Give each of the children the opportunity to ask the others their questions.

● Talk about how you find the information to answer the questions.

Assessment *(AF 2)* Can children both ask and answer simple questions about the story?

Speaking, listening and drama activities

Objective Act out stories using voices for characters (4.2).

C *(Imagining)* Let the children role-play the story of Princess Sophie.

- Explore different voices for each of the characters: *How does Sophie speak? What about the king and the queen? And the animals?*

- Once the children are 'in character', challenge them to finish the story. What happens next?

Assessment *(AF 6)* Can children act out the play using appropriate voices?

Writing activities

Objective Compose and write simple sentences independently to communicate meaning (11.1).

C *(Predicting)* Ask children to think about the ending for Anneena's story.

- Let them draw the ending, then tell you what happens before writing it.

Assessment *(Writing AF 1)* Can children write interesting endings to the story?

The Missing Crystal

> **C** = Language comprehension   A = Assessment
>
> **W** = Word recognition   O = Objective

Guided or group reading

Phonic Focus:

New graphemes for reading: /igh/ igh, –i–e, y, –ie–; /i/ –y; /ur/ –ir, er, ear, ur
Alternative pronunciations: "o" in *hot, gold;* "i" in *wind, find*
High frequency words: called, asked, very

Introducing the book

W Can children read the title? Do they know that *y* can sometimes sound like /i/? Help them to use syllables to read the title together: *Miss-ing Crys-tal*. Can they show you the two different ways of showing /i/?

W Turn to page 1. How many words can they find that include the sound /i/? (*Biff, Wilma, film, it, in Egypt, missing, crystal*). Can they identify which letters represent the sound each time?

C *(Predicting)* Encourage children to use prediction: *Where might the crystal have come from? Will it be found?*

Look through the book, talking about what happens on each page. Use some of the high frequency words as you discuss the story (see chart on page 4).

Strategy check

Remind the children to sound the words out carefully, remembering that there are different ways of showing sounds and that there are different ways of pronouncing letter patterns. Encourage them to read whole words. If they need to sound out, can they use syllables?

Independent reading

Ask children to read the story aloud. Praise and encourage them while they read, and prompt as necessary.

C *(Clarifying)* Ask children to tell you how Kipper lost his chimp.

Assessment   Check that children:

- *(AF 1)* use phonic knowledge to sound out and blend the phonemes in words (see chart on page 3).
- *(AF 1)* recognize different ways of representing /i/ and also different ways of pronouncing it.
- *(AF 2 and 3)* use comprehension skills to work out what is happening.
- *(AF 1)* make a note of any difficulties the children encounter and of strategies they use to solve problems.

Returning to the text

W Can children tell you words in which /i/ represented an unusual sound? (find) And in which /o/ represented an unusual sound? (gold)

Assessment   *(AF 1)* Discuss any words the children found tricky and talk about strategies used.

Group and independent reading activities

Objective   Recognize and use alternative ways of pronouncing the graphemes already taught (5.1).

W **You will need:** flashcards showing the words: *hot, cold, pot, post, old, gold, lost; fin, find, win, wind, kind, chill, child, will, wild.*

- Show children the flashcards. Can they sort them so that each vowel sound is in a separate pile?
- Talk about the spelling patterns. Which letters follow the long vowel pronunciations of each grapheme? (*post, child*)

Assessment   *(AF 1)* Can children recognize words where *i* and *o* are pronounced as long vowel phonemes?

Objective   Recognize and use alternative ways of spelling the phonemes already taught (5.2).

W Read page 14 aloud to the children. Ask them to raise their hands when they hear a word with the phoneme /ur/ (*bird, heard*).

- Ask children to write the words from the book and to draw sound buttons to show the phonemes. (*b-ir-d; h-ear-d*).
- Can children tell you any other ways of representing the sound? (e.g. *ur* in *hurt*, *er* in *her*). Use phoneme frames to spell the words showing /ur/ in a different colour.

Assessment *(AF 1)* Can children read and spell the words successfully?

Objective Apply phonic knowledge and skills to reading words that are not completely decodable (5.5).

W Look at page 10 together and point out the word *wasn't*. Ask the children how to say the word. Why do they think so?

- Explain that the *n't* is a short way of writing *not* and that the apostrophe shows where a letter has been taken away. Can children tell you what the long form of *wasn't* might be?
- Look at the speech bubble on page 9. Can children read it? What would the long form of *what's* be? Which letter has been taken away?
- Can children find any more examples where letters have been missed in a word and replaced by an apostrophe? (*Let's, didn't*)

Assessment *(AF 1)* Can children read and understand the words each time?

Objective Identify the main events and characters in stories (7.4).

C *(Questioning)* How many main characters are in the story? Is one more important than the others?

- Put the children into pairs (or small groups). Ask each pair to focus on one of the girl characters: Biff, Wilma, Kalila. Each pair needs to think about why their character might be the most important.
- In turn, let the pairs justify why their character is most important by explaining what they did. The other children can then ask questions.
- Can the whole group agree on who is the most important character?

Assessment *(AF 4)* Can children find reasons to explain why their character is important?

Speaking, listening and drama activities

Objective Explore familiar themes through role play (4.1).

C *(Imagining)* Use small world toys or dressing up props.

- Create the setting for a story and start to create characters thinking about why they are in the setting, whether they are goodies or baddies etc.

- Establish the idea that some kind of treasure goes missing.

- What will the children's characters do? How will they respond?

Assessment *(AF 6)* Can children participate in developing and extending a known theme?

Writing activities

Objective Use key features of narrative in their own writing (9.2).

C *(Imagining)* Give children a handout on which you have written the beginning of the story you all agreed, up to the point where the treasure goes missing.

C Ask children to continue the story, showing what happened after that point.

Assessment *(Writing AF 3)* Can children organize and present whole texts effectively, sequencing and structuring information, ideas and events?

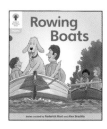

Rowing Boats

> **C** = Language comprehension   **A** = Assessment
>
> **W** = Word recognition   **O** = Objective

Guided or group reading

Phonic Focus:

New graphemes for reading: /oa/ oa, oe, o–e, ow, o; /oi/ oi, oy
Alternative pronunciations: "y" in *yes, by, very*
High frequency words: asked, their, oh, could, called, came, here, by, very

Introducing the book

W Can children read the title?

Do they know that *ow* can also sound like /oa/? Help them to sound out the title together: *R-ow-i-ng B-oa-t-s*. Can they show you the two different ways of showing /oa/?

W Turn to pages 2–3. How many words can they find that include the sound /oa/? (*rowing, boats, coats*). And /oi/? (*Joy, choice*) Can they identify which letters represent the sounds each time?

C (*Predicting*) Encourage children to use prediction: *What might happen if this group of people go rowing?*

Look through the book, talking about what happens on each page. Use some of the high frequency words as you discuss the story (see chart on page 4).

Strategy check

Remind the children to sound the words out carefully, remembering that there are different ways of showing sounds and that there are different ways of pronouncing letter patterns. Encourage them to read whole words. If they need to sound out, can they use syllables?

Independent reading

Ask children to read the story aloud. Praise and encourage them while they read, and prompt as necessary.

(C) *(Clarifying)* Ask children to tell you how they all got soaked.

Assessment Check that children:

- *(AF 1)* use phonic knowledge to sound out and blend the phonemes in words (see chart on page 3).
- *(AF 1)* recognize different ways of representing /i/ and also different ways of pronouncing it.
- *(AF 2 and 3)* use comprehension skills to work out what is happening.
- *(AF 1)* make a note of any difficulties the children encounter and of strategies they use to solve problems.

Returning to the text

(W) Can children find words in which *y* makes different sounds? (*by, suddenly*)

Assessment *(AF 1)* Discuss any words the children found tricky and talk about strategies used.

Group and independent reading activities

Objective Use knowledge of common inflections in spelling such as *plurals, ly* (6.4).

(W) **You will need:** flashcards showing the words: *boat, row, coat, stone, annoy, voice, try, float, go, soak, sudden,* and the suffixes: *ing, ly* and *s*.

- Show children the flashcards.
- Ask them to make words by adding the suffixes to the words.
- Talk about whether the words change their meaning when the suffix is added.

Assessment *(AF 1)* Can children say a sentence containing the word without the suffix and then containing the word with the suffix?

Objective Recognize and use alternative ways of pronouncing the graphemes already taught (5.1).

(W) Show the digraph *ow*. Ask children to tell you how to pronounce it. Can they tell you two ways and give words to illustrate each way? (e.g. *how, show*)

- Do the same for *o*. How many different ways can the children think of pronouncing *o*? (e.g. *to, go, Floppy, London*)
- Repeat for *y*. (e.g. *by, yes, crystal, Floppy*)

- Talk about strategies needed for reading words when there is some doubt about how to pronounce a grapheme (e.g. trying the word by saying both of the pronunciations and seeing which one sounds right).

Assessment *(AF 1)* Can children recognize that some graphemes are pronounced in different ways in different words?

Objective Spell new words using phonics as the prime approach (6.1).

W Re-read the book together.

- Model how to do dictation from the book. Read a sentence, then re-read it word by word, giving children time to write it down. Remind them to use phonics when they write some of the less familiar words.

- Ask children to work in pairs. One child in each pair should dictate a sentence from the book while the other writes it down. The children should then swap roles.

- You can look for evidence of phonic strategies being used as the children both write and spell.

Assessment *(AF 1)* Are children using phonics as the prime strategy for spelling?

Objective Recognize the main elements that shape different texts (7.4).

C *(Summarizing)* Give each pair of children three post-it notes.

- Ask children to discuss where to put the post-its in the book, to mark the most important events.

- Talk about where the different pairs put their post-its. Were they all in the same place? What was the same or different?

- Agree as a group where you would put the post-its to mark the three most important events.

Assessment *(AF 4)* Can children justify their decisions about where the important events occurred?

Speaking, listening and drama activities

Objective Explore familiar themes through role play (4.1).

C *(Questioning)* Tell children they are going to hot-seat one of the characters in the story. Let each child choose a different character.

- Give all of the children time to look through the book again to see what their character does, and to think about what they want to ask the others.
- Let the children work in groups of three or four as they hot-seat their different characters.
- Talk about what the children found out about the characters during the hot-seating.

Assessment *(AF 3)* Can children both ask and answer questions about a character's role in the story?

Writing activities

Objective Write chronological texts using simple structures (10.1).

C *(Imagining)* Ask children to write about one important event in the book from the point of view of the hot-seated character.

- Share write one event to model writing in the first person. Add a sentence to show a reaction to the event.

Assessment *(Writing AF 1)* Can children write an imaginative response to the event?

Mr Scroop's School

> **C** = Language comprehension   **A** = Assessment
>
> **W** = Word recognition   **O** = Objective

Guided or group reading

Phonic Focus:

New graphemes for reading: /oo/ oo, u–e, ue, ew, ui, ou; /er/ er, e, a, o
Alternative pronunciations: "ow" in *how, gown, now*; and in *show, showed*
High frequency words: Mr Mrs called asked oh could their don't very your time(s)

Introducing the book

W Can children read the title?

Check they recognize the high frequency word: *Mr.*
Help them to sound out the title together: *Mr S-c-r-oo-p-'s- S-ch-oo-l.*

W Turn to pages 2–3. How many words can they find that include the sound /uoo/? (*to, new, shoes, school*). Can they identify which letters represent the sounds each time?

C *(Clarifying)* Pause on pages 2–3 and check what children already know about life in Victorian times.

Look through the book, talking about what happens on each page. Use some of the high frequency words as you discuss the story (see chart on page 4).

Strategy check

Remind the children to sound the words out carefully, remembering that there are different ways of showing sounds and that there are different ways of pronouncing letter patterns. Encourage them to read whole words. If they need to sound out, can they use syllables?

Independent reading

Ask children to read the story aloud. Praise and encourage them while they read, and prompt as necessary.

C *(Clarifying)* Did the children like Mr Scroop's school by the end of the story?

Assessment Check that children:

- *(AF 1)* use phonic knowledge to sound out and blend the phonemes in words (see chart on page 3).
- *(AF 1)* recognize different ways of representing /oo/ and also different ways of pronouncing it.
- *(AF 2 and 3)* use comprehension skills to work out what is happening.
- *(AF 1)* make a note of any difficulties the children encounter and of strategies they use to solve problems.

Returning to the text

W Can children find words in which *ow* makes different sounds? (e.g. *showing*, *now*)

Assessment *(AF 1)* Discuss any words the children found tricky and talk about strategies used.

Group and independent reading activities

Objective Recognize and use alternative ways of spelling the phonemes already taught (5.2).

W Play 'Phoneme Spotter'. You read two or three pages of the book aloud, asking children to raise their hands when they hear an /oo/ word.

- Read the pages again, while the children follow in their book. Give children time to note down /oo/ words.
- Ask children to sort the words into groups, each group featuring a different way of representing /oo/

Assessment *(AF 1)* Can children identify and sort the words correctly, isolating the letters needed to represent /oo/ each time?

Objective Read and spell phonically decodable two syllable and three syllable words (6.5).

(W) Ask children what strategies they would use to spell the word 'Victorians'. Encourage them to think in terms of representing the word syllable by syllable: Vic-tor-i-ans.

- Ask children to work in pairs: in each pair, one child should say the word while the other tries to listen to the vowel phonemes in each syllable. Can they find the spelling that is used for /er/ in the final syllable? (*a*)

- Repeat for the words: *children, teacher, history*. Can children identify the spelling of the /er/ vowel? (child-r<u>e</u>n, teach-<u>er</u>, hist-<u>o</u>-ry).

Assessment *(AF 1)* Can children recognize different ways of representing the unstressed /er/ vowel?

Objective Recognize and use alternative ways of pronouncing the graphemes already taught (5.1).

(W) Show children the grapheme *ow*. Ask them how many ways they know of pronouncing it. (as in *now* and *show*)

- Ask children to look for different ways of representing each kind of '*ow*' (e.g. *how* and *shout; show* and *told*)

Assessment *(AF 1)* Are children able to use alternative ways of pronouncing the graphemes?

Objective Distinguish fiction and non-fiction texts and the purposes for reading them (8.3).

(C) *(Clarifying)* Ask children to look through the book and see what they can learn about life in Victorian times.

- If possible, use the internet and books from the school library to verify the facts you have identified.

- Compare the books and web sources used. Talk about how you would recognize this book as fiction and other books as non-fiction. Find and list features to look for. Discuss when you might choose to look at each of the different types of books.

Assessment *(AF 6)* Can children recognize the different types of books and the purposes for reading them?

Speaking, listening and drama activities

Objective Re-tell stories, ordering events using story language (1.2).

  C *(Summarizing)* Ask children to think about what Chip and his friends will tell their Mums about their visit to Mr Scroop's school.

  ● Let them work in pairs to list the main events and summarize to identify the most important experiences.

  ● Ask each pair to share their ideas with the rest of the group.

Assessment *(AF 4)* Can children summarize the experiences of the characters by identifying the main events?

Writing activities

Objective Compose and write simple sentences independently to communicate meaning (11.1).

  C *(Imagining)* Ask children to imagine they are Chip or Biff. What will they write for the class book about their day at Mr Scroop's school?

  ● Encourage children to work using ICT if possible, to make the activity more realistic.

Assessment *(Writing AF 1)* Can children communicate their intended meaning clearly?

The Haunted House

> **C** = Language comprehension **A** = Assessment
>
> **W** = Word recognition **O** = Objective

Guided or group reading

Phonic Focus:

New graphemes for reading: /or/ au, aw, al, or, our; /oo/ ou, oo, u, o;
/o/ (w)a, o

Alternative pronunciations: "c" in *cellar, could;* "a" in *that, what*

High frequency words: oh asked don't house saw old here very

Introducing the book

W Can children read the title?

Check that they know that /or/ can also sound like *aw*. Help them to sound out the title together: *The H-au-n-t-e-d H-ou-se*

W Turn to pages 1–5. How many words can they find that include the sound /or/? (*August, Dawn, door, ball, caught, naughty*) Can they identify which letters represent the sounds each time?

C (*Prediction*) What do the children think the title of the book means? *Is there any indication on pages 1–5 that the house may be haunted? What might happen there?*

Look through the book, talking about what happens on each page. Use some of the high frequency words as you discuss the story (see chart on page 4).

Strategy check

Remind the children to sound the words out carefully, remembering that there are different ways of showing sounds and that there are different ways of pronouncing letter patterns. Encourage them to read whole words. If they need to sound out, can they use syllables?

Independent reading

Ask children to read the story aloud. Praise and encourage them while they read, and prompt as necessary.

C *(Clarifying) Was the house haunted? Why did the children think it was?*

Assessment Check that children:

- *(AF 1)* use phonic knowledge to sound out and blend the phonemes in words (see chart on page 3).
- *(AF 1)* recognize different ways of representing /or/ and know that o can be pronounced in different ways.
- *(AF 2 and 3)* use comprehension skills to work out what is happening.
- *(AF 1)* make a note of any difficulties the children encounter and of strategies they use to solve problems.

Returning to the text

W Can children find words in which o makes different sounds?

Assessment *(AF 1)* Discuss any words the children found tricky and talk about strategies used.

Group and independent reading activities

Objective Recognize and use alternative ways of pronouncing the graphemes already taught (5.1).

W Show children the grapheme o. Ask them how many ways they know of pronouncing it (as in *Floppy, to, go, woman*).

- Ask the children to hunt for o words in the book. Check that they don't include o as part of another grapheme. Write the o words and ask children to say how o is pronounced. Group the words you find.

Assessment *(AF 1)* Are children able to group the o words to show different pronunciations?

Objective Recognize and use alternative ways of spelling the phonemes already taught (5.2).

W Children can play 'Phoneme Spotter' in pairs, taking it in turns to read and to listen out for the phoneme /or/. The listener should raise their hands when they hear an /or/ word.

- Children should re-read the book in pairs, noting down all of the /or/ words they find.

- Ask children to sort the words into groups.

Assessment *(AF 1)* Can children identify and sort the words correctly?

Objective Spell new words using phonics as the prime approach (6.1).

- **W** Ask children to remind you of the graphemes they found which represent /or/. Display them all.

- Tell children you're going to say some /or/ words. Can they decide which of the graphemes they need in each word?

- Say: *haunted, taught, four, your; ball, hall, talk; paw, claw.*

Assessment *(AF 1)* Can children spell words using different ways of representing /or/?

Objective Visualize and comment on ideas making imaginative links to their own experiences (8.2).

- **C** *(Clarifying)* Draw a representation of Kipper with two thought bubbles. In the second thought bubble, write the words 'Paula's band'.

- Ask the children what you should write in the first bubble. Explain that the first bubble should be about what Kipper thought the noise was.

- Can the children tell any anecdotes about their own experiences where they made a mistake and thought that one thing was something else? If they can't think of anything from real life, can they think of any ideas?

Assessment *(AF 6)* Can children make links between the theme of the book and their own experience?

Speaking, listening and drama activities

Objective Explore familiar themes and characters through improvisation and role play (4.1).

- **C** *(Imagining)* Re-read pages 16–19.

- Let the children work in pairs or threes, to create a short role play showing something else Kipper *might* have seen when he opened the door. They could base their role plays on the ideas you have already discussed, or on new ones.

Assessment *(AF3)* Can children act out appropriate suggestions?

Writing activities

Objective Independently choose what to write about, plan it and follow it through (9.1).

C *(Imagining)* Ask children to write a new end to the story, showing what Kipper might have seen instead when he ran through the doors.

- Encourage them to plan their writing by drawing a picture. They can use the drawing for ideas.

- They can write on paper or on screen.

Assessment *(Writing AF 2)* Can children produce texts that are appropriate to task, reader and purpose?